AR 3.8 / 0.5   620L

www.abdopublishing.com

Published by Abdo Publishing, a division of ABDO, PO Box 398166, Minneapolis, Minnesota 55439. Copyright © 2015 by Abdo Consulting Group, Inc. International copyrights reserved in all countries. No part of this book may be reproduced in any form without written permission from the publisher. Big Buddy Books™ is a trademark and logo of Abdo Publishing.

Printed in the United States of America, North Mankato, Minnesota.
092014
012015

THIS BOOK CONTAINS RECYCLED MATERIALS

Cover Photo: Getty Images.
Interior Photos: ASSOCIATED PRESS (pp. 5, 9, 15, 17, 19, 21, 23, 25, 27, 29); Collegiate Images/Getty Images (p. 11); Getty Images (p. 13); Ron Sachs/picture-alliance/dpa/AP Images (p. 7).

Coordinating Series Editor: Rochelle Baltzer
Contributing Editors: Bridget O'Brien, Marcia Zappa
Graphic Design: Maria Hosley

Library of Congress Cataloging-in-Publication Data

Tieck, Sarah, 1976-
  Russell Wilson : Super Bowl champion / Sarah Tieck.
    pages cm. -- (Big buddy biographies)
  ISBN 978-1-62403-574-6
 1. Wilson, Russell, 1988- --Juvenile literature. 2. Football players--United States--Biography--Juvenile literature. 3. Quarterbacks (Football)--United States--Biography--Juvenile literature. I. Title.
 GV939.W545T54 2015
 796.332092--dc23
 [B]
                                  2014026441

Russell Wilson

Contents

Football Star 4
Family Ties 6
Young Talent 8
School Years. 10
Starting Out. 12
Minor Leagues 14
Strong Finish 18
NFL Player 20
Growing Stronger. 22
Super Bowl Winner 24
Off the Field. 26
Buzz 28
Snapshot 30
Important Words 31
Websites. 31
Index 32

> **Did you know...**
> Russell's name on Twitter is @DangeRussWilson. So, sometimes people call him "Dangeruss."

Football Star

Russell Wilson is famous for his sports skills. He plays football in the National Football League (NFL). Russell is a talented, popular **quarterback** for the Seattle Seahawks.

In 2014, Russell helped the Seahawks win the Super Bowl!

Family Ties

Russell Carrington Wilson was born on November 29, 1988. His mother is Tammy Wilson. His father was Harrison Wilson III. Russell's older brother is Harrison IV and his younger sister is Anna.

Russell grew up in Richmond, Virginia. There, his father worked as a **lawyer**. His mother worked in nursing.

Russell and his family are close. In 2014, he took his mother to the White House Correspondents Association Annual Dinner.

Did you know...

Russell's dad and grandfather both played football in college. They helped Russell become a strong athlete.

Young Talent

Russell grew up in an athletic family. His grandfather saw how he played with a bat and ball. He told the family that Russell would do great things in sports.

Russell began playing football at age four. He continued to improve his skills by practicing throwing with his brother.

Today, Russell's throwing ability is one of his strongest game skills.

School Years

Russell played football, baseball, and basketball at Collegiate School in Richmond. There, he became known for his strong arm. He helped the Collegiate Cougars win three state football **championships**!

As a junior, Russell was honored as an all-state, all-region, and all-district football player. In 2005, he was named the *Richmond Times-Dispatch* Player of the Year.

Russell's hard work in high school helped him do well in college.

Starting Out

Colleges noticed Russell's talent. Russell got **scholarship** offers from two schools. He chose to attend North Carolina State University (NC State). There, he studied **communications**. He played baseball and football for the NC State Wolfpack.

Russell spent many hours practicing football. It paid off! During his second year, he became the team's starting **quarterback**. Russell continued to stand out for his strong throwing arm.

Russell (*number 16*) made a good addition to the Wolfpack.

Minor Leagues

Russell enjoyed playing football for NC State. But, he also wanted to play **professional** sports. In 2010, Russell was **drafted** to play baseball for the Colorado Rockies.

Russell's father died in 2010 after Russell was drafted by the Rockies. This time was both sad and happy for Russell. His family helped him. And, he grew in his faith.

Did you know...

Professional baseball players often start in the minor leagues. There, they strengthen their skills. As players improve, some move on to Major League Baseball.

Russell attended spring training with the Rockies. During the summer, he played minor league games.

The football coach at NC State wanted Russell to focus on football. Russell wanted to do both. So in 2011, he left to play football for the University of Wisconsin–Madison Badgers. The coach there didn't mind if Russell played baseball, too.

Russell played minor league baseball for the Asheville Tourists (*pictured*) and the Tri-City Dust Devils.

Did you know...

In 2011, Russell set Big Ten records. This included most passing yards per attempt and most passing touchdowns.

Strong Finish

Russell proved to be a strong addition for the Badgers. He set several single-season school records.

The Badgers made it to the Rose Bowl in January 2012. This would be Russell's last college football game. The Badgers played well but lost to the Oregon Ducks. Now, Russell looked to the NFL.

Russell was excited to play in the Rose Bowl. Each year, the top two college football teams play this game in Pasadena, California.

NFL Player

In 2012, Russell entered the NFL **draft**. He had shown his skill in college. But, some people thought he wouldn't play well in the NFL. He is smaller than many other players.

The Seattle Seahawks chose Russell in the third round of the draft. People expected Russell to be the backup **quarterback**. Instead, he became starting quarterback before the 2012 season began!

Russell's first season with the Seahawks was in 2012. His skill took fans by surprise!

Growing Stronger

In 2012, Russell threw 26 touchdown passes. This tied the NFL **rookie** record! Russell led the Seahawks to an undefeated home record! He was named the Pepsi Max Rookie of the Year.

By 2013, the Seattle Seahawks were considered one of the top NFL teams. People expected Russell and his team to continue to play well.

Russell is very popular. He takes time to meet fans.

Super Bowl Winner

The 2013 season went well for the Seahawks. They made it to the play-offs. The Seahawks won all their play-off games. This meant they would play in the Super Bowl.

In 2014, Russell led the Seahawks to their first-ever Super Bowl win! They beat the Denver Broncos 43–8. The Seahawks received a Vince Lombardi Trophy.

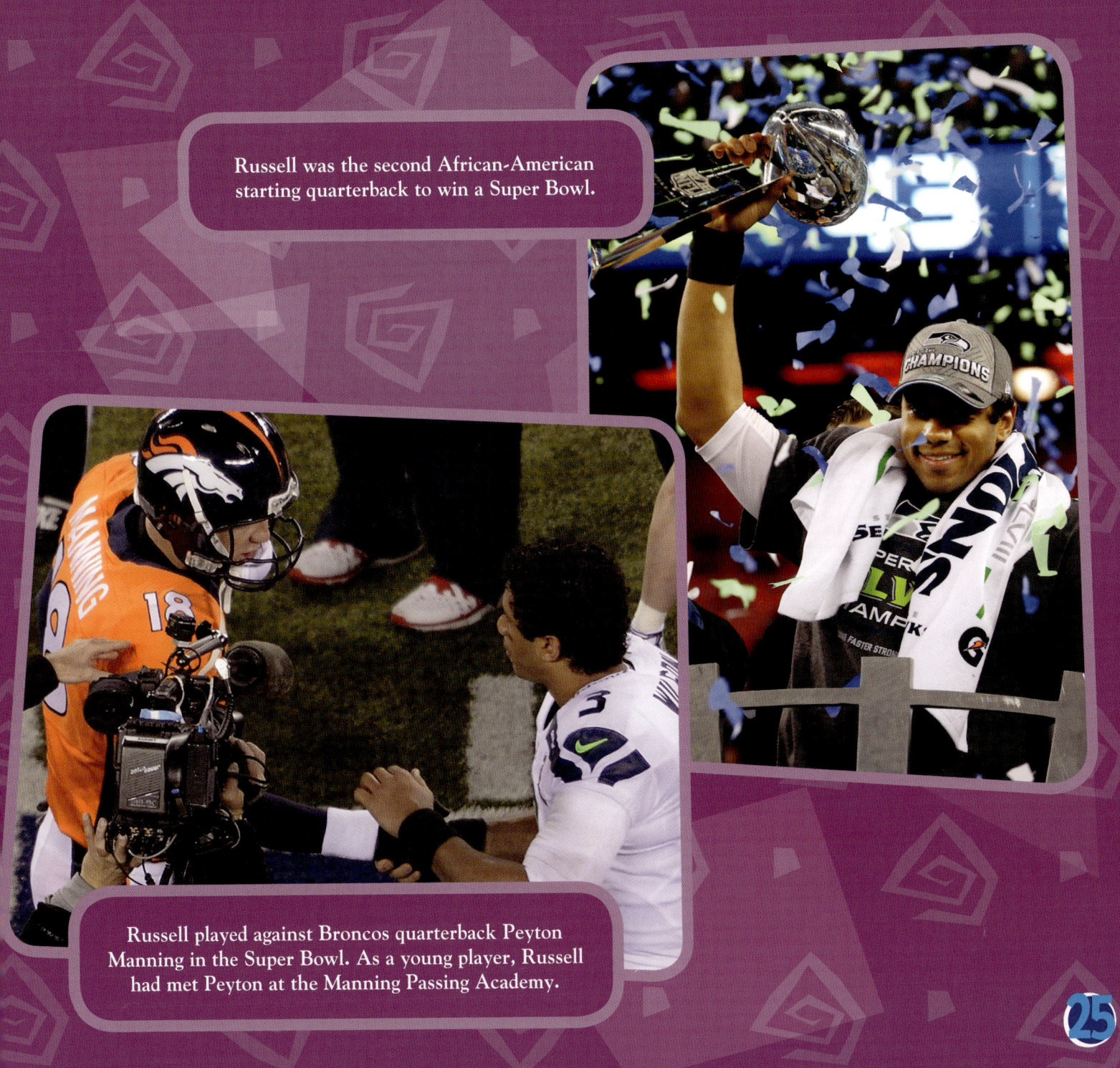

Russell was the second African-American starting quarterback to win a Super Bowl.

Russell played against Broncos quarterback Peyton Manning in the Super Bowl. As a young player, Russell had met Peyton at the Manning Passing Academy.

> **Did you know...**
> Russell supports the Power of Mind Foundation. This group helps provide activities for kids in need. For example, it sends kids to the Russell Wilson Passing Academy.

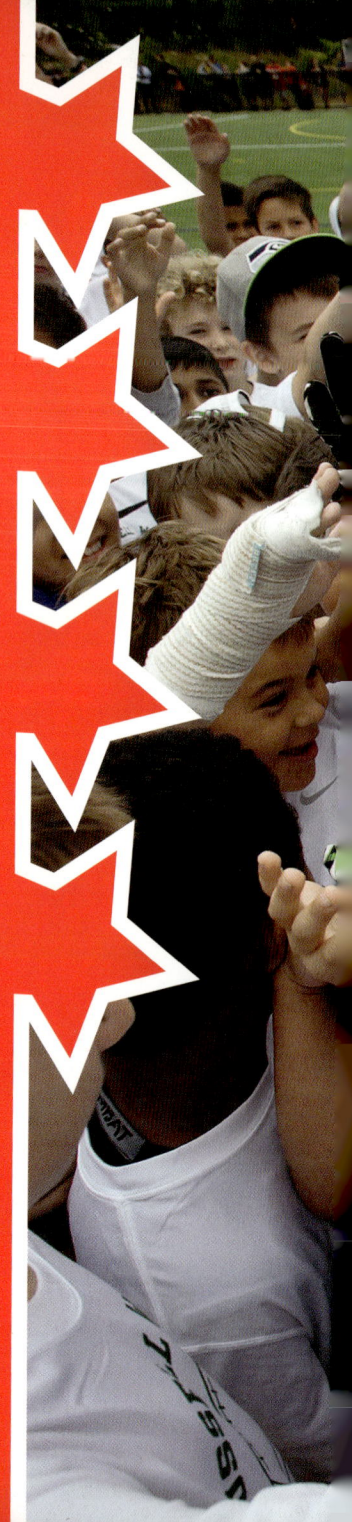

Off the Field

In 2012, Russell started a football camp for kids ages 9 to 17. It is called the Russell Wilson Passing Academy. Russell also uses his fame to help others. Sometimes, he visits children in hospitals.

The Russell Wilson Passing Academy helps kids build strong values.

Did you know...

In December 2013, Russell joined the Texas Rangers. This is a Major League Baseball team. Russell said he had a goal of being a two-sport professional athlete.

Buzz

Russell was thrilled when the Seahawks won the 2014 Super Bowl. He looked forward to his third season with the team.

Russell continues to work hard. Fans are excited to see what's next for Russell Wilson!

Russell is a team leader. He helps encourage other players during practice.

Snapshot

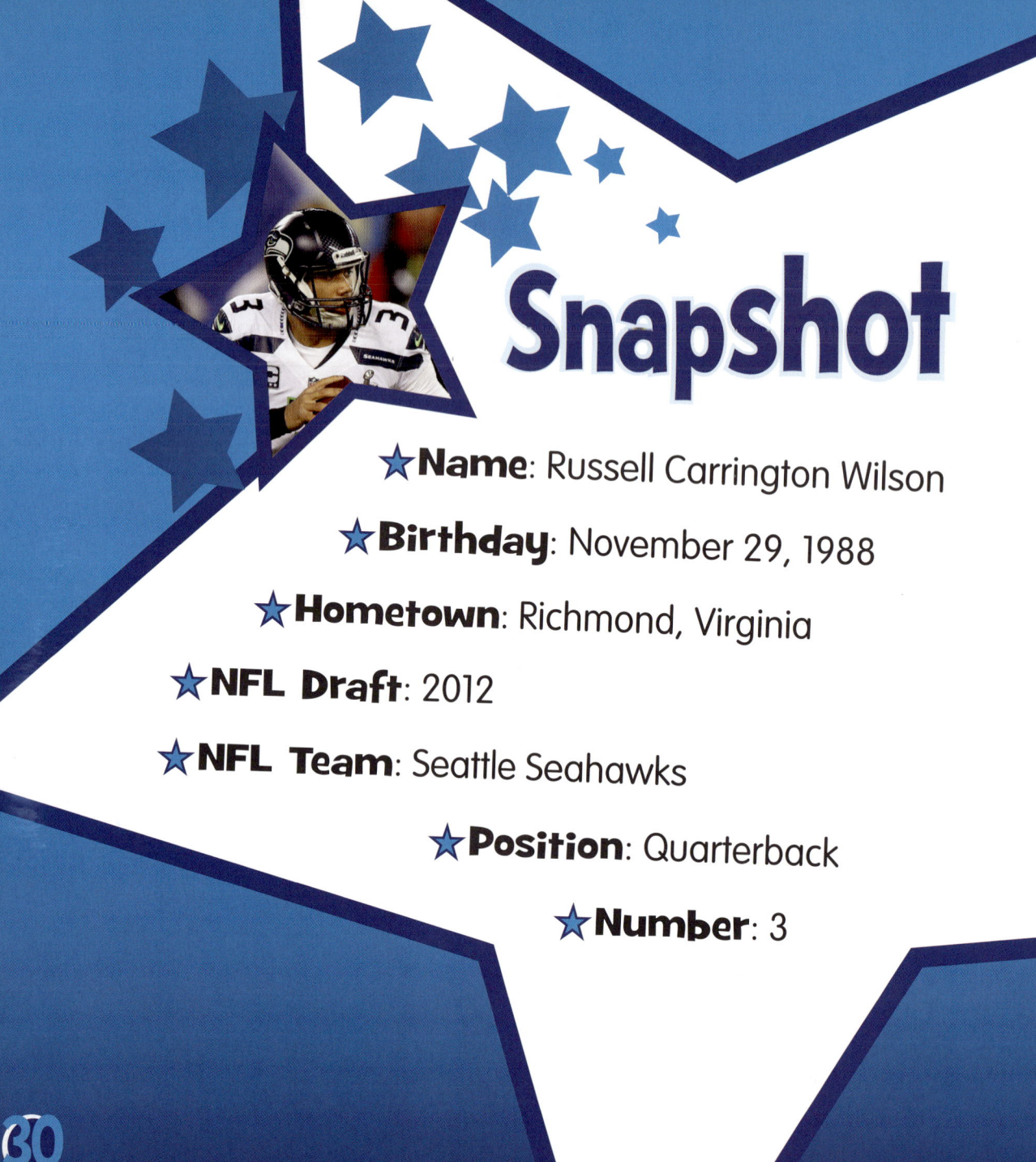

★ **Name**: Russell Carrington Wilson

★ **Birthday**: November 29, 1988

★ **Hometown**: Richmond, Virginia

★ **NFL Draft**: 2012

★ **NFL Team**: Seattle Seahawks

★ **Position**: Quarterback

★ **Number**: 3

Important Words

championship a game, a match, or a race held to find a first-place winner.

communications the study of how knowledge or news is given to people.

draft a system for professional sports teams to choose new players. When a team drafts a player, they choose that player for their team.

lawyer (LAW-yuhr) a person who gives people advice on laws or represents them in court.

professional (pruh-FEHSH-nuhl) working for money rather than only for pleasure.

quarterback a football player who calls signals and directs the offensive play of a team. Quarterbacks are often known for their throwing skills.

rookie a first-year player in a professional sport.

scholarship money or aid given to help a student continue his or her studies.

Websites

To learn more about Big Buddy Biographies, visit **booklinks.abdopublishing.com**. These links are routinely monitored and updated to provide the most current information available.

Index

Asheville Tourists **17**

awards **10, 22**

California **19**

charity work **26**

Colorado Rockies **14, 15, 16**

Denver Broncos **24, 25**

education **10, 11, 12**

Major League Baseball **16, 28**

Manning, Peyton **25**

National Football League **4, 18, 20, 22, 30**

North Carolina State University Wolfpack **12, 13, 14, 16**

Oregon Ducks **18**

Power of Mind Foundation **26**

Rose Bowl **18, 19**

Russell Wilson Passing Academy **26, 27**

Seattle Seahawks **4, 5, 20, 21, 22, 24, 28, 30**

Super Bowl **5, 24, 25, 28**

Texas Rangers **28**

Tri-City Dust Devils **17**

University of Wisconsin–Madison Badgers **16, 18**

Virginia **6, 10, 30**

Wilson, Anna **6, 7, 8, 15**

Wilson, Harrison, III **6, 7, 8, 15**

Wilson, Harrison, IV **6, 7, 8, 15**

Wilson, Harrison, Jr. **8**

Wilson, Tammy **6, 7, 8, 15**

DISCARD'